FATHERHOOD

When Ceilings Become Floors

Anthony L. Winans

DEDICATION

First and foremost, to **God** —

The true and perfect Father. Thank You for never leaving me, even when I tried to do it all on my own. You saw the brokenness I tried to bury and patiently walked me through the healing I didn't know I needed. You tore down ceilings I built out of pain and turned them into the floors I now stand on. Every word in this book was breathed from the grace You've shown me.

To my eldest son, **Anthony Winans** —

Thank you for inspiring this book. Through the rebuilding of our relationship, God revealed the hidden ceilings in my heart that I didn't even know were there. Your life, your presence, and even the tension between us became the mirror God used to show me what healing looks like. I love you, and I'm proud of who you are.

To my younger sons, **Aiden and Austin Winans** —

This was written with you in mind. My prayer is that these words give you more than memories but they offer a model. My desire is that you two know what it means to walk in sonship, wholeness, and identity, not just as men, but as beloved sons of God.

To my father, **Charles Underwood** —

Even in your absence, I honor your life and the legacy that shaped mine. God has used your presence and your passing to bring clarity, compassion, and peace to my journey. I thank God for the impact you still have on me today.

And to my uncle, **Oscar Jones** —

Thank you for being a consistent, tangible reflection of the Father's heart. Every time you called me "son," a piece of my hardened heart softened. God used you as both voice and vessel to help me experience what I missed and to believe in what's still possible.

This is for every man still becoming. Every son still healing. Every father still building. And the God who redeems it all.

Acknowledgments

To my amazing wife, **Aries Winans**—thank you for staying on me and believing in me through every step of writing this book. Your patience, your affirmations, and your encouragement were what helped me navigate through uncertainties. You didn't just support me you championed me. I love you deeply, and I'm grateful for your love and support.

To my aunt, **Crystal Jones**—thank you for always seeing the gift in me, especially when I couldn't see it in myself. You pull the talent out of me with love, honesty, and grace. You challenge me, but never without covering me. Your words push me forward, and I receive them with gratitude and respect.

And last but certainly not least, to my mother, **Joyce Underwood**—I'll never forget the prayers you prayed when I was hurting for the presence of my father. One prayer has never left me: *"God, be the Father to him that he doesn't have right now."* Ma, He heard you and He answered! Thank you for standing in the gap, for praying when I couldn't, and for never giving up on your son.

CONTENTS

Dedication...iii

Acknowledgments v

Introduction... ix

Chapter 1: The Chair in My Mother's Room 1

Chapter 2: The Ceiling I Didn't Know I Built 9

Chapter 3: You're On Your Own 17

Chapter 4: Becoming a Son Again 23

Chapter 5: Letting the Father Be My Father......................... 31

Chapter 6: No Cap, Just Kingdom 39

Chapter 7: The Strength of Being Seen 45

Chapter 8: Rebuilding from the Rubble 53

Chapter 9: Building Beyond the Ceilings 59

Ending Prayer: A Yes to the Rebuild 65

Ways to Identify Hidden Ceilings in Your Life....................... 66

INTRODUCTION

Fatherhood: When Ceilings Become Floors

If you've ever experienced any kind of distance from your father, whether he left when you were young, passed away before you were born, refused to acknowledge you, or was physically present but emotionally unavailable, then you know the weight that kind of absence can leave behind. It's not always loud. Sometimes it's subtle, like the way you flinch at vulnerability, or the way you measure your worth by what you produce. That kind of pain has a way of shaping us, especially as men. We take that experience and, without realizing it, start building ceilings…low ones. Ceilings made of survival, of toxic strength, of unspoken grief. Ceilings that define how we see ourselves, how we love, how we parent. And because we might be doing "better" than what we came from, we assume we're healed. We assume we're whole. But better doesn't always mean healthy.

This book is for the father still trying to figure it out, and the son still trying to recover from what wasn't there. It's for every man who's ever thought, "I'll never do to my kids what was done to me," not realizing that even that vow, noble as it sounds, might be rooted in unaddressed hurt. This isn't about shaming the effort or dismissing the accomplishments. It's about exposing the hidden ceilings we've built out of pain and offering the hope that God doesn't waste the rubble. He wants to turn what capped us into something we can build on.

The truth is, many of us are walking around with an identity shaped by false definitions of manhood and fatherhood. But God wants to heal that. He wants to reveal who you are as a son before you ever pick up the mantle of being a father. No matter your age, I believe there's a ceiling in your life that you've subconsciously accepted as normal but God's ready to tear it down and give you something solid to stand on.

This is my story... a story still being written. It's a journey of unlearning, and healing. It's about trusting God enough to stop building with the broken bricks I inherited. And I believe God is ready to take your hand, too, not just to fix what was broken, but to walk with you as you become the kind of man, the kind of father, you were always meant to be. All He needs is a *yes*.

CHAPTER 1

THE CHAIR IN MY MOTHER'S ROOM

When Pain Became the Blueprint

I was nine years old when my father left. There's a certain stillness that creeps into a home when a presence suddenly becomes an absence. It's not just about someone no longer being around, it's the silence that follows…broken promises and unanswered questions. I can still see myself hopeful at any type of interaction with him. I would get drawn into the idea that he'd be coming shortly to pick me up, waiting anxiously for him to show up. "I'll come get you this weekend," he'd tell me, his voice full of plans and pretend certainty. And sometimes, he did. But most times, he didn't. The promises fell empty. The day would pass. And I'd quietly retreat to my room, pretending I was okay. But one day, at the age of 16, the weight of all those broken promises broke me. I remember sitting in my mother's room, slumped in a recliner with the old school knitted blanket draped across the back. It was the chair that my Dad often sat in when he was living with us. I couldn't hold it in anymore. I buried my face into my hands, drenched in disappointment, I cried. Through my tears I said words I never forgot: "Why don't he want me?" I know that's not the proper way to say it but that's

1

exactly how it came out. It wasn't anger in that moment. It was pure, raw hurt. The kind of hurt that doesn't worry about sounding right, because it just wants to be heard. The hurt of a boy becoming a man too soon. The hurt of wanting to be seen, wanted and loved by my dad. From that day forward, I stopped chasing after the idea of reconciliation. I built a wall, not made of bricks, but of bitterness and unspoken expectations. A quiet hatred crept in, not loud or violent, but cold and calculated. I didn't speak ill of him. I was raised to be respectful and cordial. But inside? He became a ghost, alive, but irrelevant. If someone told me he passed away, I wouldn't have flinched. I felt he didn't add or subtract from my life. He was a zero. But the truth was I still wanted him. I still needed that 16-year-old question answered. "Why don't he want me?"

Becoming a Father Myself

Years later, life brought me full circle. I became a father. I remember the moment my son was born, how the world seemed to pause as I held him for the first time. His fingers curled around mine like he was already reaching for something I didn't yet know how to give. I stared down at him in wonder, feeling both an overwhelming joy and a quiet fear I didn't want to admit. That day, I made silent vows in my heart: I will be there. I will show up. I will not leave him like my father left me.

In those early years, fatherhood felt like redemption. Every birthday party I attended, I tried to be present in my son's life as best as I knew how. Each moment felt like I was reclaiming ground my own father had abandoned. I convinced myself that I was breaking the cycle. But then my son turned nine. Nine. That number hit me like a punch to the chest. I didn't expect it. I hadn't prepared for it. But something shifted in me. A scary uncertainty began to whisper beneath my confidence. It was as if I had been sprinting through fatherhood, full of passion and purpose, only to suddenly hit a wall I didn't know was there. It was the same age I was when my father left. I started questioning myself in ways I never had. What do I do now? What does fatherhood look like beyond this point? My instincts no longer felt sharp. My confidence wavered. I was present, but unsure, still holding his hand, but now uncertain of the direction. Even though my son was raised in a separate household I assumed my promise keeping was the proof that I hadn't left him or forgotten him. That's when I realized something profound: I had unknowingly set a ceiling over my own fatherhood, the age where my dad left was where my blueprint ended. I had no model beyond that point. Everything past the age of nine was foreign territory. In my mind, I measured my progress by my father's absence rather than by my child's needs. I'm still here. I didn't walk out. That must mean I'm doing well... right? But the truth was sobering - not leaving isn't the same as leading. I had confused better with healed. I had mistaken endurance for wisdom.

The unspoken ceiling, the silent limit I had placed on myself was still intact. And because I hadn't confronted it, I began to parent from a place of insecurity, masked as effort. I assumed masculinity to be more like a mask-u-lent-to-me; my identity was questionable while hidden behind a made-up idea of a leader.

What I didn't realize at the time was that I had become a man walking in the shadow of pain rather than the light of purpose. My pain had shaped my path, and until I dealt with it, I couldn't truly guide my son past where my father had stopped guiding me.

> IN MY MIND, I MEASURED MY PROGRESS BY MY FATHER'S ABSENCE RATHER THAN BY MY CHILD'S NEEDS

Forgiveness- The Turning Point

Eventually, God began to deal with me about my father. I had carried unforgiveness for so long, I didn't realize it had settled into the way I thought, loved, and parented.

The Lord says in Ephesians 4:31-32:

"Let all bitterness, and wrath, and anger, and clamour, and evil speaking, be put away from you, with all malice: And be ye kind one to another, tenderhearted, forgiving one another, even as God for Christ's sake hath forgiven you.

I didn't want my son to inherit the weight of what I hadn't forgiven. So one day, I packed up my son and told him we were going to visit his grandfather. I hadn't seen my dad in years. The plan wasn't just to say hi. It was to lay down the pain, to let my son see what forgiveness looks like, not just in theory, but in motion. We sat across from my father while we were out having ice cream. I began to speak slowly, hesitantly, at first. My voice cracked as my heart poured out. I told him about the broken promises. The hurtful expectations. The birthdays that came and went without a call. I confessed the hatred I carried, not loud or spiteful, but cold and calculated. Then, after a long pause, I looked him in the eye and said, "But today... I forgive you." With a steady gaze I could tell he was processing everything that was said. He looked down at the table, then back at me. He took a deep breath, and said, "Son... I'm sorry." Those words held weight; decades of silence broken in a sentence. He went on to tell me how he had struggled during that time. He admitted he was dealing with addiction, drowning in shame, trying to escape his own pain. In so many words I gathered he was saying, "I wasn't running from you," he said. "I was running from myself." Hearing his heart didn't erase the hurt, but it did something powerful, it gave context to the chaos. It didn't excuse what happened, but it explained the brokenness behind it. And for the first time, I saw my father not just as the man who failed me, but as a man who had been fighting demons of his own. And just like that, God began to heal what years of distance couldn't. Forgiveness didn't happen in one moment; it started in one. It was the beginning of restoration. Of redemption. Of reshaping what fatherhood meant for me and what legacy could look like for my son.

The Rebuild and the Redemption

From that day on, we began rebuilding. Not in a rush. Not with forced smiles or pretending the past hadn't happened. But slowly. Intentionally. Brick by brick, word by word, moment by moment. We spoke more often. We'd end phone conversations with him saying he loved me, something I had longed to hear as a boy. And now, as a grown man, those simple words began to soothe places in me that had been calloused over for years. He began showing up, not just in word, but for life. There was a weight to his presence now, not because he was perfect, but because he was *present*. And that mattered more than he probably realized.

He began affirming me in my adulthood, noticing the man I had become and speaking into who I was growing into. He'd say things like, "I'm proud of you," or "Keep up the good work," and those words did something in me that no award ever could. They rewrote a silent narrative I had carried for too long. But healing isn't always a straight line. When I got married, rejection crept back in like an unwelcome guest. Deep down, I had hoped my dad would be there, standing with me, blessing this new chapter of my life. I imagined what it would be like for him to meet my bride, shake my hand as a man, maybe even offer a word of wisdom before I said, "I do." But he didn't come. That old feeling of abandonment came rushing back. The 9-year-old in me stood in the corner of my heart, whispering, See? Nothing's changed. He still doesn't show up. I had a choice, either bury the disappointment like I used to, or face it with the honesty God had been teaching me. So I brought it up. We talked about it. And that conversation marked another turning point. Unlike the past, when I would suppress, minimize, or spiritualize my pain. This time, I leaned into it. And so did he. He apologized again. He explained his reasoning. And we

> FORGIVENESS DIDN'T HAPPEN IN ONE MOMENT; IT STARTED IN ONE

resolved it, not by pretending it didn't hurt, but by surrendering it to God. James 5:16 says, *"Confess your faults one to another, and pray one for another, that ye may be healed."*

That's what we did. And as God continued to work in both of us, our relationship grew deeper. He began calling just to share Scripture. Sometimes, he'd leave me voicemails quoting something the Lord had spoken to him in prayer and studying. When I accepted the call to be a pastor, he became one of my greatest encouragers. He didn't just support the title, he supported me. He spoke into me, reminding me of who I was in God. Proverbs 16:24 says, *"Pleasant words are as an honeycomb, sweet to the soul, and health to the bones."* That's what his encouragement became for me, healing. Sweetness. Life-giving.

Three years into our reconciliation, my father passed away. But the man who died wasn't the one who abandoned me. He was the one who returned, who took accountability, who made the call, who gave the apology. He was the man who embraced the son he once left behind and made peace before the clock ran out. He was the man I had learned to admire. Respect. Even love. And though our time was brief, God did a quick work, not just in him, but in me. I no longer saw him as a zero, a shadow, or a symbol of my pain. I saw him as a redeemed man who, at the end, became someone I was proud to call Dad.

It reminds me of Joel 2:25, where God says: *"And I will restore to you the years that the locust hath eaten…"* God didn't give us back time, He gave us back relationship. And in the end, that was the miracle I didn't know I needed.

7

CHAPTER 2

THE CEILING I DIDN'T KNOW I BUILT

Breaking Old Patterns, Building New Presence

The Age I Feared Most

Reconciliation with my father before he passed was meaningful, but it didn't erase the emotional fear that crept in when my own son turned nine. That number haunted me. Nine was the age my dad walked out of my life and left my mom behind too. It wasn't just fatherhood that became unfamiliar territory for me after that age. It was manhood. It was marriage. His absence didn't just create a void; it redefined my expectations of what life as a man might look like. I had no blueprint. I had no model of what it meant to remain present when life got hard.

Eventually, I did grow to recognize good examples, godly men who loved their wives, raised their children with patience, and stood firm in faith. These men showed me what godly masculinity could look like in action. They were strong, gentle, present, and prayerful. But here's what I didn't realize then: you can admire a healthy example and still be governed by a wounded experience. The examples helped, but they didn't automatically heal what had been formed deep within me. The resolve I made as a child, *"never be like him"* was still shaping my choices. That vow was made in pain, not promise. And it left me measuring my success by avoidance instead of alignment with God's design. So, as my son approached that same age nine, I felt the shadow of fear rising in me. I didn't walk away. I stayed. I provided. I showed up when called. In my mind, that made me a better man than my father had been. But even though I didn't leave my son physically, something emotional began to drift. He was leaning into his own identity, finding his voice, becoming his own person. And I assumed we were fine. I told myself: He's thriving. He's respectful. We're good. I was proud of him. I celebrated his achievements. But in truth, I was leaning into his success more than our connection. I had confused

> YOU CAN ADMIRE A HEALTHY EXAMPLE AND STILL BE GOVERNED BY A WOUNDED EXPERIENCE

presence with intimacy. I was still measuring fatherhood by how far I'd come from the pain I knew, rather than the health of what we had. And that's when I started to notice the ceiling. A subconscious ceiling had been set, the kind not built on faith, but on fear. Not based on God's truth, but on my own internal wounds. A ceiling that said, "If I make it past where my father failed, then I'm good." But better isn't always whole.

When Time Moves, But the Heart Stays Still

Time didn't wait. Life kept rolling forward. My son graduated high school and entered college, and with that came a new season of pride and admiration. He was stepping into adulthood with grace, doing the things a father longs to see his son do achieving, growing, handling responsibilities. On paper, it looked like legacy. In my heart, though, something didn't sit right. Every time I congratulated him or posted a photo, I felt proud, but I also felt distant. There was no drama between us, no blow-up moment or harsh words. He was always respectful, always kind. If you judged our relationship by tone and timing, we passed the test. The hugs were real. The "I love yous" were said. We communicated. But it was like speaking through glass. I could see him, but not feel him. Conversations started to feel like check-ins rather than connections. His decisions grew more independent, and while I knew that was part of manhood, I couldn't ignore how familiar it all felt. The distance wasn't just new, it was old. It felt like me at sixteen. I remembered how I slowly disengaged from my father. Not in open rebellion, but with quiet resolve. I learned to stop needing him. I adjusted my expectations downward and lived accordingly. That same quiet detachment was beginning to echo in my relationship with my own son. I had to ask myself: Was I witnessing the same story, told in a different voice?

The Appearance of Health vs. the Absence of Depth

From the outside, we looked like a strong father-son pair. People would say: "You two have a great relationship." We had the right pictures. The right posture. Even the occasional vulnerable moment. But I knew the difference between presence and participation. And my spirit could feel the gap. So I asked the question. "Son, have I done anything to offend you?" He would look me in the eyes, kind and composed, and say, "No, Dad. We're fine." But it wasn't fine. It was familiar. The same calm tone I once used to protect my own pain. The same silent smile I used to wear so my father wouldn't ask questions I wasn't ready to answer. It was like watching a replay of my younger self, only this time I was the father. I tried to rationalize it. "He's just like me," I told myself. "I'm not overly expressive. Maybe he's wired that way too." But the Holy Spirit gently interrupted that excuse.

The Truth Behind My Silence

"Why aren't you more engaging?" That question hit me hard. It wasn't about personality. It was about conditioning. I realized I had been trained by trauma. I had been taught to manage emotions alone and to internalize pain. I was taught to "man up" and move on. I learned not to trust vulnerability, especially with other men. The silence I once thought was strength was actually a symptom. A scar. And that same silence, no matter how unintentional, may have communicated something damaging to my son, something I never meant to say: "You're on your own." That realization broke me. Because deep down, I knew what that message felt like. As a teenager, I used to ask myself, "Why don't he want me?" And suddenly I had to consider the terrifying possibility, Maybe my son had asked that about me. Not because I was absent, but because I was emotionally unavailable. I did not intentionally reject him, but I wasn't present with him in the moments that mattered most. I wasn't running away from him, but inside I was still hiding.

"Search me, O God, and know my heart: try me, and know my thoughts." -Psalm 139:23, KJV

I had to stop measuring my fatherhood by effort alone. I had to take inventory not just of what I provided, but of who I was. This was the moment when the internal ceiling came into full view. God had not built this ceiling. It was installed by the enemy through fear, hurt, and unspoken trauma. By this time, I was married, leading a church, working full time and raising more children. My calendar was full. My responsibilities were many. From the outside looking in, it looked like I was doing

> THE SILENCE I ONCE THOUGHT WAS STRENGTH WAS ACTUALLY A SYMPTOM. A SCAR.

everything right. But a full schedule doesn't equal wholeness in soul. I realized I had been moving forward without addressing that part of me that still felt unfinished. I had assumed that my physical presence was enough for my son. I believed that if I showed up, helped financially, supported dreams, and offered advice when asked, I was succeeding as a father. But God started to deal with the ceiling I had unknowingly placed over fatherhood.

The ceiling I had inherited said:

- "If you're better than your father, you're a good dad."

- "If they're not complaining, they're fine."

- "If they're successful, your job is done."

But God began to expose the cracks in that thinking. Because those ceilings weren't set by Him. They were set by pain, survival, and comparison.

The Men's Conference That Became a Mirror

In an intentional effort to reconnect, I invited my son to a men's conference. It felt like a step forward. We worshiped together. Laughed. Talked. We were shoulder to shoulder in God's presence, and for the first time in a long while, it felt like the gap was closing. But I couldn't ignore what I'd learned before, that proximity doesn't always mean intimacy. So, after the trip, I paused. I looked him in the eyes and asked again: "Son, is there anything I've done to hurt you?" This time, I added something deeper: "I know I haven't always been the best dad. I know I could've done better." That moment broke the surface.

> BUT A FULL SCHEDULE DOESN'T EQUAL WHOLENESS IN SOUL

With honesty and respect, he began to share his heart. He wasn't bitter. He told me how, at times, he felt left out. He said it in a way that had me visualize it as if he was peeking into a family he was disqualified from. It wasn't that he didn't feel loved. But he noticed there was a difference. To him, it felt like he was watching a version of me that he had once longed for, but wasn't fully able to receive. That pierced my heart. Because I knew what it was like to watch a father from a distance and wonder: "Why not me?"

The Moment the Ceiling Was Redefined

That conversation changed everything, not just between us, but inside me. I had always assumed that my improvements were enough to cover the pain. I never meant to hurt him. I thought my growth was evidence that I had broken the cycle. But cycles don't just break with behavior, they break with truth. And here's what I realized: I wasn't failing by being imperfect. I was failing by pretending imperfection didn't exist. The ceiling I had created over fatherhood was too low.

It was built on:

> BUT CYCLES DON'T JUST BREAK WITH BEHAVIOR, THEY BREAK WITH TRUTH

- Avoidance, not intention.
- Survival, not healing.
- Comparison, not calling.

And that ceiling was affecting both of us. So, I did what I had to do: I repented to God and to my son. I admitted my failures. And I made space for his pain, and for his process. I learned healing isn't just about being forgiven. It's about building something new together.

A Kingdom Floor, Not a Cultural Ceiling

As I began to rebuild, God gave me language for what had been happening all along. I wasn't just a father raising a son. I was a man reclaiming my identity. The ceiling I had placed was built on accomplishments, my son's grades, his maturity, his outward respect. But God showed me that His model for fatherhood wasn't based on performance, it was based on presence, pursuit, and grace.

"And be not conformed to this world: but be ye transformed by the renewing of your mind..." -Romans 12:2, KJV

Renewing the mind meant letting go of the old metrics. The world said: provide, protect, perform. God said: connect, cover, and be present. The shift wasn't just in my parenting; it was in my perspective. This journey with my son became a blueprint for how God was fathering me. I remembered what I gathered from my dad through the forgiveness process in our later years: "I wasn't running from you. I was running from myself." And now, I could say the same. My addictions didn't look like his, but the cycle was still there, running from emotional closeness, hiding behind ministry, measuring worth by wins. It had to stop. Today, my son and I are rebuilding. There are no shortcuts. No easy answers. But now we're building on truth, not tension. A new foundation, one made of grace, humility, transparency, and love. A kingdom floor, not a cultural ceiling.

> THE WORLD SAID: PROVIDE, PROTECT, PERFORM. GOD SAID: CONNECT, COVER, AND BE PRESENT

"My grace is sufficient for thee: for my strength is made perfect in weakness." -2 Corinthians 12:9, KJV

I've learned that true masculinity isn't about masking your pain, it's about inviting God into it. It's not "Mask-u-lent-to-me" it's "Father, show me who You say I am."

CHAPTER 3

YOU'RE ON YOUR OWN

How One Lie Shaped My Manhood, and God Undid It

The Lie That Lingered

Before a rebuild, there has to be a demolition. When everything safe, familiar, and strong began to fall, I noticed the walls I had been living behind. One of them stood taller than the rest. Its name: "You're on your own." It wasn't loud. It didn't shout. It whispered, quietly and consistently, in moments of pain, rejection, and confusion. That wall had been there since I was sixteen, sitting in my mother's room, tears burning my face, asking, "Why don't he want me?" I never said the phrase, "I'm on my own" out loud, but I lived it every day. It framed how I showed up in the world. It told me to protect myself. It convinced me to depend on no one. It helped me survive, but it also kept me from healing. That wall looked strong. It had been holding up everything I thought made me a man: independence, achievement, resilience. But when God began calling me to rebuild, not just as a father but as a son, I had to make a hard choice. No matter how strong those walls had been, I couldn't use them again. They weren't made for what God was building. Because what I called strength, God called isolation. What I called protection, He called pride. And before I could build something new, I had to let Him tear down the old.

When the Wall Followed Me Into Fatherhood

That wall didn't just stand in my teenage years; it followed me into adulthood. It shaped how I loved, how I led, and how I lived. I didn't call it trauma. I called it drive. I didn't call it abandonment. I called it ambition. I had no blueprint for vulnerability with other men because "You're on your own" had taught me not to need anyone. I wasn't just building a life; I was building a fortress. Brick by brick, accomplishment by accomplishment, I proved to myself that I could succeed without a father, without support, without covering. I graduated. I provided. I succeeded in ministry. I became what my father never was for me. From the outside, it looked like healing. But on the inside, I was still driven by the hurt of a boy asking, "Why didn't he choose me?" "You're on your own" taught me not to cry in front of anyone. It taught me to keep conversations shallow, relationships transactional, and emotions buried. Even when I had community around me, I felt like I had to carry the weight myself. I loved people, but I didn't let anyone see me bleed. That lie that I was alone was still setting the limits for how I fathered, how I trusted, and how I prayed. Even after forgiving my father, even after reuniting with my son, that wall tried to find its way back into the new build. It was subtle, showing up in my hesitation to ask for help, in my need to always be the strong one, in my fear of truly being known. I didn't realize that every time I leaned into that fear, I was reusing the same bricks I told God

I'd leave behind. But here's the truth I couldn't see back then: I was never alone. That night when I sat crying in my mother's room, asking why...God was there. When I made reckless choices, looking for comfort in the streets and in women...God was there. When I numbed my pain with performance and buried it under ministry...God was still there. It wasn't that God wasn't speaking. It's that my trauma was louder than His truth. The lie had a voice, and I mistook it for reality. But even in my confusion, God kept pursuing me through every act of protection I didn't deserve, every person who loved me past my walls, every quiet moment when I felt something whisper, You're not alone. That whisper was Him.

Trading Isolation for Intimacy

It wasn't my idea to go to my father for forgiveness. Let me say that plainly, I didn't want to. Everything in me had settled into the belief that I had moved on. That I didn't need closure, didn't need answers, didn't need him. But that wasn't healing. That was survival, not wholeness. The day I felt prompted to reach out to him wasn't wrapped in a spiritual high. It was quiet. A gentle nudge in my spirit that I couldn't shake. I knew it wasn't me; I had made peace with the wall. But God hadn't. He was determined to finish what He started in me. This wasn't about my father's apology. It was about my heart, and my

> IT WASN'T THAT GOD WASN'T SPEAKING. IT'S THAT MY TRAUMA WAS LOUDER THAN HIS TRUTH

19

surrender. I was nervous. And then I was angry. And underneath all that, I was terrified. Because if I let this wall fall, what would I stand on? But that's when God reminded me: You're not standing on your own. I've been holding you this whole time. So we made the trip. I didn't have a script. I just had a choice to be honest and vulnerable. It was time to say what my sixteen-year-old self never got to say. And when I told my father how I felt, how his absence shaped me, how it left me feeling unwanted, God gave me the courage to speak through the pain. And more than that, He gave me the strength to stay soft. That was the miracle. Not that we resolved everything in one conversation, but that I chose truth over protection. I was not alone. God was right there with me. Years later, I'd need that same courage again. This time, not as a son, but as a father, when my own son started to pull away, subtly at first, then more obviously. I began to see reflections of myself in him: the same silent anger, the same emotional distance, the same inner question I once asked, "Why don't he want me"? And just like before, that old lie crept back in: You're on your own. Fix it yourself. But God interrupted again. He reminded me that what I needed as a son is what I must now offer as a father: presence, not perfection. So I didn't wait for my son to come to me. I pursued him. I apologized. I listened. I owned my failures and offered him the one thing I had once longed for, a safe place to be vulnerable.

> HE REMINDED ME THAT WHAT I NEEDED AS A SON IS WHAT I MUST NOW OFFER AS A FATHER: PRESENCE, NOT PERFECTION

And in doing that, I saw the grace of God unfold in real time. I saw the wall start to fall, not just in my life, but in his.

The New Blueprint: Fathered By God

Rebuilding couldn't start until I was willing to leave the old bricks behind. And as I let those walls fall, the walls of self-made strength, isolation, and silent suffering, I saw what was left underneath. It wasn't weakness or failure. It was space for God to build something new. The lie of "You're on your own" had kept me from trusting, depending, and allowing myself to be fathered by God. It was a strong wall, one that helped me survive. But like I said before, survival isn't the same as healing. It's not the same as love.

God didn't just want to heal the hurt; He wanted to show me a different blueprint. He reminded me that His fatherhood doesn't resemble the broken patterns I'd seen or lived through. His foundation is different. It's not built on my ability to succeed or protect or prove. It's built on presence. His presence. The same presence that met me when I cried in that chair in my mother's room at sixteen. The same presence that whispered, "I do." I didn't recognize Him then, not through the noise of pain, pride, and pretending. But He was there. And He has never left. When I stepped into reconciliation with my father, God was there. When I struggled to reach my son and fight off the shadows of my own past, God was there. When I felt like a failure and feared I'd repeat the cycle, God was still there, patient, faithful and present. So now I build differently. Not on control, but on connection. Not on silence, but on honesty. Not on pride, but on grace.

This isn't a cultural ceiling, this is a kingdom floor. A foundation rooted in the truth that I am not alone, have never been alone, and never will be.

And if I can teach my children anything, it's that:

- You don't have to build walls to be strong.

- You don't have to hide to be loved.

- You don't have to walk alone.

Because your Father is here.

CHAPTER 4

BECOMING A SON AGAIN

Learning to Be a Son Changed the Way I Father, Lead, and Live

Breaking through this cultural ceiling and building on this kingdom floor wasn't found in manhood alone… but in sonship. God was after a complete demolition. And in the rubble, He handed me something I had never fully understood: the identity of a son. 1 John 3:1 (NIV) says, *"See what great love the Father has lavished on us, that we should be called children of God! And that is what we are!"* This wasn't just about healing old wounds, it was about re-learning how to live. The truth is, a healthy father is first a healthy son. If I couldn't receive God as my Father, how could I model that to my own children? Sonship is not a reward for good behavior. It's a position we're invited into. And that changes everything. As a man shaped by fatherlessness, I carried a silent pressure to perform. I needed to prove I belonged and that I was enough. Even when I said I trusted God, I often lived like He was distant, like He expected me to handle everything and only check in when I was falling apart. That's not sonship. That's slavery.

> SONSHIP IS NOT A REWARD FOR GOOD BEHAVIOR. IT'S A POSITION WE'RE INVITED INTO

"The Spirit you received does not make you slaves, so that you live in fear again; rather, the Spirit you received brought about your adoption to sonship. And by him we cry, 'Abba, Father.'"
—Romans 8:15 (NIV)

THE FATHER DIDN'T WANT MY PERFORMANCE; HE WANTED MY HEART

The Father didn't want my performance; He wanted my heart. He wanted my tears, my questions, my weakness, my surrender. And in exchange, He offered presence, identity, and covering. Learning how to be a son meant learning how to trust again. That was the hardest part. Trust meant I had to stop managing everything on my own. It meant I had to accept love without earning it. It meant asking for wisdom, for help, for grace without shame. This wasn't passive; it was powerful. It was how Jesus Himself lived. *"...I do nothing on my own authority, but speak just as the Father taught me." – John 8:28.* Even Jesus, the perfect Son, showed us what it looked like to live in total dependence on the Father. He wasn't less of a man for it, He was the model of manhood because of it. So if Jesus needed the Father, how could I think I didn't?

From Isolation to Inheritance

The cultural ceiling taught me a lot of things: strength was isolation, real men didn't cry, leaders don't need accountability, and vulnerability is a liability. But sonship showed me the opposite: my greatest strength is found in my surrender. My

24

covering is not a crutch, it's my confidence. When I began to embrace my identity as a son, I could lead my family differently. I wasn't leading from fear or insecurity. I was leading from inheritance. I didn't have to make my sons feel small to feel strong. I didn't need perfection to prove my worth. I could listen. I could repent. I could say, "I don't know, but I'll ask my Father." That posture changed everything. The greatest gift I can give my children is not just provision or protection, it's a model of what it looks like to be fathered by

> THE GREATEST GIFT I CAN GIVE MY CHILDREN IS NOT JUST PROVISION OR PROTECTION, IT'S A MODEL OF WHAT IT LOOKS LIKE TO BE FATHERED BY GOD

God. My sons and daughter don't need to see a man who never struggles, they need to see a man who knows where to go when he does. They need to watch me pray, cry out, and trust God. They need to see me receive. Because here's the truth: sons become fathers and daughters gauge manhood from what's been modeled in front of them. And if I don't teach my boys how to be sons first, they'll repeat the same cycle I had to break. The old ceiling said, "Be a man." God said, "Be My son." The old walls said, "You're on your own."

God said, "I will never leave you nor forsake you." The rebuild doesn't begin with grit, it begins with grace. It starts when we stop trying to prove something and begin to receive what God has for us. We become the fathers our children need when we first become the sons our Father designed us to be.

Becoming a Son Changed How I Saw the Father

Before I truly understood sonship, I saw God the way I had experienced earthly fatherhood, inconsistent, distant, and hard to please. I saw Him as someone I had to earn approval from. When life went wrong, I assumed I had messed up and now He was disappointed. When I succeeded, I hesitated to celebrate because I thought it was only a matter of time before I failed again. My idea of God was wrapped in performance and punishment, not in love and relationship. That's what happens when your identity is shaped by fatherlessness. You create a version of God based on the ceiling you've known, one that says "Don't mess up," "Handle it yourself," or "You're on your own." But something shifted when I started learning what it means to be a son.

"The Lord is compassionate and gracious, slow to anger, abounding in love... As a father has compassion on his children, so the Lord has compassion on those who fear Him."
—*Psalm 103:8,13 (NIV)*

As I began to embrace God, not just as Lord but as Father, my heart softened. My posture changed. I no longer approached Him like a servant approaching a harsh boss. I came as a son approaching a loving Dad. I realized He wasn't waiting to punish me, He wanted to embrace me. I didn't have to perform, I just had to come to Him. When I lived with the mindset of "I'm on my own," I prayed like I was on my own. My prayers were short, transactional, survival-mode. I asked for help, but didn't expect comfort. I asked for provision, but didn't expect presence. I talked to Him like He was far away. But the more I accepted that

I was His son, the more I understood He was never distant, I just didn't know how to draw near. James 4:8 says, *"Draw near to God, and He will draw near to you."* I began to see the Father not as someone whose approval I had to chase, but as the One who had always

> THE MORE I ACCEPTED THAT I WAS HIS SON, THE MORE I UNDERSTOOD HE WAS NEVER DISTANT

pursued me. He wasn't absent, He was always there. I was the one who had built walls of independence so high I couldn't see His face.

It reminds me of the story of the prodigal son (Luke 15:11-32). The son left home thinking he had to find his own way, build his own life, and prove himself apart from his father's covering. He didn't realize that in trying to be independent, he was actually walking away from the one place where love wasn't earned, it was given. When he finally came to the end of himself, he said to himself, "I'm no longer worthy to be called your son." But the Father wasn't interested in the false perception he made of himself. He ran to meet him, embraced him, and restored him, not because the son got it all right, but because the Father never stopped loving him. That story became my story. I realized I had spent years approaching God like a hired hand, thinking I had to prove myself before I could be embraced. But like the prodigal, I found that the moment I turned toward Him, He was already running toward me, ready to cover, comfort, and call me "son."

Trusting the Father's Heart

A true son doesn't just obey the Father's commands; he trusts the Father's heart. That was the part I had to relearn. I could follow God, do ministry, and still be emotionally distant from Him. But a son doesn't just work for the Father, he walks with Him. The more I trusted His heart, the more I realized everything He does is out of love. His discipline wasn't rejection, it was correction. His delays weren't silence; they were strategy. His "No" wasn't neglect, it was protection. I had to (and am still) address the misconception I formed in my mind on the treatment I received from a father.

> A TRUE SON DOESN'T JUST OBEY THE FATHER'S COMMANDS; HE TRUSTS THE FATHER'S HEART

That's when God, in His grace, brought my uncle into the picture, someone who didn't just show up, but showed love in a way that started breaking through walls I didn't even know were still standing. I'll never forget the time I made the reckless decision to drive without a license, ended up miles from home, and had to call him in desperation. I was expecting judgment, disappointment, maybe even silence. But instead, he came with no anger, no lecture, just presence. He picked me up and made me feel like I was still worth showing up for. That moment stayed with me. It didn't seem loud, but it echoed deeply. He called me "son" long before I believed I was one. And every time he said it, something in me softened. That steady love started dismantling the walls I had built out of pain and pride. My uncle became the tangible echo of what God had been whispering all along: I was never fatherless. I wasn't alone. I was simply unaware of how covered I really was. Through him, God began to rewrite what fatherhood meant not just through words, but through consistency, compassion, and care. It made room in me to finally receive what I had always needed most: the love of the Father.

"Which of you, if your son asks for bread, will give him a stone?... If you then, though you are evil, know how to give good gifts to your children, how much more will your Father in heaven give good gifts to those who ask him!"
—Matthew 7:9–11 (NIV)

That Scripture hit different when I began to view God not as a judge, but as a Dad. A perfect Dad. One I could trust even when I didn't understand. One who wasn't afraid of my tears,

> WHEN YOU BECOME A SON, GOD STOPS BEING A THEOLOGICAL CONCEPT AND BECOMES ABBA DADDY. INTIMATE. PRESENT. PERSONAL

my mess, or my silence. When you become a son, God stops being a theological concept and becomes Abba Daddy. Intimate. Present. Personal.

And as my view of Him changed, so did everything else:

- My prayers became conversations.
- My worship became response, not ritual.
- My identity became secure, not scattered.
- My fatherhood became modeled, not manufactured.

I could now see that He wasn't just God over me, He was Father with me. He fathered me through every failure. Covered me in every collapse. Held me in every heartbreak. And now, as I father my own children, I know that I'm not drawing from emptiness, I'm reflecting the fullness of what I've received. I don't just want to be a father who provides, I want to be a father who reflects the heart of the One who never left me.

CHAPTER 5

LETTING THE FATHER BE MY FATHER

How I Unlearned Performance and Received Love Without Earning It

I didn't just have to become a son again, I had to learn how to be fathered. There's a difference. Becoming a son sounds poetic and powerful. It's a call to identity. But letting the Father be my Father? That was intimate, vulnerable and hard. You see, I had my own definition of what love from a father looked like. And it wasn't rooted in grace; it was grounded in performance. Somewhere between my father leaving and me trying to make sense of the silence, I internalized a belief: love had to be earned. If I did something impressive enough, maybe I'd get noticed. If I performed just right, maybe I'd finally be worthy. Maybe I'd be embraced.

This mindset didn't disappear just because I grew up, became a father, and gave my life to God. It stayed with me, silently shaping how I received love, even from Him. Yes, I had forgiven my dad. Yes, I had found peace before he passed. I loved him again, and truly believed we were good. But as I got closer to God, He began unlocking hidden doors I didn't know were still shut. Resentment I thought was buried. Expectations I thought were healed. Insecurities I thought were resolved. All still there. God wasn't punishing me. He was parenting me.

He was showing me how to love deeper by first showing me the parts of me that still didn't know how to receive it. He wasn't asking me to perform, but He was asking me to trust and that was the stretch. The hard truth? I had no problem becoming His son. My real struggle was letting Him be my Father. That meant letting Him into places I had guarded for decades. It meant asking myself uncomfortable questions:

- Can I trust Him with my heart?

- Will He still love me if I fail?

- What if He leaves too?

- What if I'm not enough without what I do?

I wouldn't have said these things out loud, but they were living loud inside of me. I was raised in a culture of hustle. We measure value by output. Success is celebrated and failure is hidden. Vulnerability gets likes online but is rare in real life. So when God came to me not with demands but with delight, not with pressure, but with presence. I didn't know how to handle it. I didn't know what to do with that kind of love. Love that doesn't require performance felt unfamiliar. Foreign, even. I could understand that from a mother, that's where I'd seen unconditional love most clearly. But a father? That was a different story. I had no blueprint. So even in my walk with God, I separated His love into categories. I believed He loved me *as a*

Christian as long as I read my Bible, did ministry and stayed away from sin. But as a Father loving His son? That felt too generous and too easy. And it exposed something: I didn't actually believe I was enough just as I was.

God began to chip away at that belief. Not with force, but with kindness. Not through loud declarations, but through quiet moments. When He loved me through my mess, not after it. When He didn't abandon me in failure. When He met me in silence and didn't demand I say the right things. When His correction didn't come to shame me, but to free me.

At first, I didn't recognize it as love. It felt like pain. Like He was picking at scabs I had learned to live with. But that's what real fatherhood does, it doesn't leave wounds untreated just because they're covered. He heals them. My natural father never really pushed me to deal with the deeper stuff. So when God started pulling out the boxes I hid under my emotional bed, it felt more like confrontation than care. But that was the lie being exposed. I thought love was supposed to feel comfortable. God showed me that real love is willing to risk your comfort for your healing.

> BUT THAT'S WHAT REAL FATHERHOOD DOES, IT DOESN'T LEAVE WOUNDS UNTREATED JUST BECAUSE THEY'RE COVERED. HE HEALS THEM

It was in those moments I realized something: I wasn't being rejected, I was being restored.

Romans 5:8 says, *"But God demonstrates his own love for us in this: While we were still sinners, Christ died for us."*

That's the kind of love I was being introduced to. Not "once you get it together" or "once you prove your worth" love. But "I loved you before you even knew how to love Me" kind of love.

> MY DEFINITION OF LOVE FROM A FATHER HAD TO DIE SO I COULD LIVE IN THE TRUTH OF WHAT IT REALLY IS

That love broke my rebellion. And it rebuilt my identity. Letting God father me meant I had to stop trying to impress Him. I had to stop hiding behind ministry or maturity. I had to let Him see the boy in me, the scared parts, the confused parts, the disappointed parts. And every time I expected Him to turn away, He leaned in. Every time I thought, "This is too much," He reminded me, "I'm not going anywhere." It turns out, the love I thought I had to earn was always freely given. I just didn't know how to receive it. But slowly, grace started to rewrite what I thought love was supposed to be. My definition of love from a father had to die so I could live in the truth of what it really is.

Letting God Father Me

Letting God be my Father didn't just change how I saw me, it redefined how I saw Him. I had always known Him as Savior, my rescue when I was lost, my peace when I was spiraling. I also knew Him as Lord, worthy of reverence, the one I was called to obey. But Father? That required a different kind of closeness and trust. The word "Father" carried some weight for me. Not just because of who my natural father was, but because of who he wasn't. Even after forgiveness, after growth, after becoming a father myself, there were still parts of me that hadn't been redefined, just ignored. Subconsciously, I built a system in my mind where love from a father had to be earned. Maybe if I impressed him, I'd get his attention. Maybe if I acted like him, he'd be proud. That logic didn't die with my father it just got quietly transferred to how I saw God. So even when I said "God loves me," there was still this unspoken feeling attached, "As long as I keep doing right."

What I didn't realize was how deeply that mindset had shaped me. It fed into people-pleasing, performance, perfectionism even in ministry. I could teach about grace but quietly panic when I felt I wasn't doing enough. I

> BUT GOD WASN'T ASKING ME TO DO MORE. HE WAS ASKING ME TO RECEIVE MORE

knew scripture that said God's love was unconditional, but in my heart, I still treated it like a rewards system. If I prayed more, fasted more, served more then maybe I'd feel worthy of it.

But God wasn't asking me to do more. He was asking me to receive more. That's where things started to shift. He wasn't trying to strip me of responsibility; He was trying to heal the way I received love. Not the transactional kind I was used to. Not the applause of people or the approval of spiritual performance. But the love of a Father who sees everything, my flaws, my past, my fear and still says, "You're mine."

That kind of love exposed parts of me I didn't know were broken. The moments where I had moved on but hadn't actually healed. The thoughts I had normalized. The pride that told me I had to hold it all together to be worth keeping around. The stuff I never said out loud, but still believed deep down. And when God started dealing with that, (I won't lie) it didn't feel like love at first. It felt like pressure. It felt invasive. But only because I had gotten so comfortable hiding those parts, I forgot they weren't supposed to stay locked away.

Letting God father me wasn't about getting cuddly and emotional. It was about letting Him touch the parts of me my own father never reached. It was Him confronting the lies I built my identity around. It was Him challenging my walls, not to break me down, but to build me up on something real. The deeper I went with God as Father, the more I saw the fullness of who He really was. Savior wasn't just about pulling me out of sin, it was about rescuing me from beliefs that had shaped how I saw love. Lord wasn't just about obedience; it was about surrendering to a kind of leadership I could finally trust.

This was new for me. Not just becoming a son, but letting God actually *be* my Father. That meant trusting His correction without assuming it meant rejection. It meant leaning into His protection without questioning His presence. It meant accepting love freely given untied to an achievement. That journey wasn't instant. It was layered. It still is. But with every layer, He keeps showing me what real love looks like and more importantly, how much of it I've always had access to.

Accepting God as my Father wasn't the finish line. It was only the beginning of the journey I believe He wanted to take me on. That realization is still wrecking me in the best way.

CHAPTER 6

NO CAP, JUST KINGDOM

Building the Kingdom Life on the Freedom of Sonship

Sonship changed everything. It wasn't just a concept; it became a lens. Once I accepted that I was a son of God, loved without performance, covered without condition, and welcomed without shame, I realized something else. I'd been building my life on blueprints that didn't come from my Father. The problem wasn't just that I had the wrong materials. It's that I thought ceilings were normal. I had learned to live with limits. Emotional ceilings. Spiritual ceilings. Generational ceilings. Ceilings that told me how far I could go, how deep I could feel, how real I could be. But the more I walked with the Father, the more I realized: there are no ceilings in the Kingdom, just unlimited sky. In the Kingdom of God, there are no spiritual, emotional, or generational limits placed on those who walk in sonship. The Kingdom offers an ever-increasing access to grace, growth, and glory, because our identity is rooted not in

> IN THE KINGDOM OF GOD, THERE ARE NO SPIRITUAL, EMOTIONAL, OR GENERATIONAL LIMITS PLACED ON THOSE WHO WALK IN SONSHIP

performance or pain, but in relationship with the Father through Christ.

"Now unto him that is able to do exceeding abundantly above all that we ask or think, according to the power that worketh in us..."
—Ephesians 3:20 (KJV)

That truth was both freeing and frightening. Because while God removed the ceiling, I still had a habit of building new ones. Even on this new road, even after the revelation of sonship, I had to face this hard truth: my heart still knew how to pick up old tools. The old tools shaped by fear, by the streets, and by a wounded childhood. It was like muscle memory. My heart still knew how to measure worth by wins, how to hide behind strength, how to resist help and call it "maturity." I wasn't tempted to go back to my old lifestyle. I was tempted to go back to being unapproachable. To parenting from performance. To preaching without transparency. That's how ceilings creep in, not through rebellion, but through routine. I had to guard my heart like never before. Because the greatest danger wasn't failure, it was success on the wrong foundation. Proverbs 4:23 says, *"Keep thy heart with all diligence; for out of it are the issues of life."*

> BECAUSE THE GREATEST DANGER WASN'T FAILURE, IT WAS SUCCESS ON THE WRONG FOUNDATION

In this season, God wasn't just tearing things down. He was teaching me how to build differently. And that required intentional, aggressive, daily work because the old model of manhood doesn't just bow out quietly.

The Ceilings I Almost Rebuilt

There were moments, even after healing, when I still caught myself reaching for the old wood. Like when my son needed grace, and I gave him pressure. Or when I didn't want to admit I was tired, because I thought needing rest meant I was weak. Or when I silently questioned God's presence in the middle of progress, as if being "used by Him" meant I didn't still need Him. I had been delivered, yes, but I still needed discipline. A Kingdom rebuild requires rejection of the old foundation. And that's painful. Especially when it worked before. The old me survived by being self-

> A KINGDOM REBUILD REQUIRES REJECTION OF THE OLD FOUNDATION

sufficient. The Kingdom me thrives by being surrendered. That's a war. God's foundation is immovable. His floor is grace, truth, sonship, presence, and identity. But what I build on top of that is up to me. Ceilings aren't imposed; they are intentional. *"For ye have not received the spirit of bondage again to fear; but ye have received the Spirit of adoption…"* —Romans 8:15 (KJV)

Fear wants to install new ceilings. Shame wants to bring back the old drywall. Culture wants me to compromise the frame. But the Spirit of adoption says, "You're free to grow. You're free to breathe. You're free to expand." And I've decided: I'm building wide. I'm building high. I'm building slowly if I have to. But I will not build with ceilings. Because the Kingdom doesn't call "cap". It calls you.

A Kingdom Without Limits

Before I could build something new, I had to recognize that I was still carrying old limitations. The walls I had built in survival, independence, toughness and silence became ceilings that kept me from receiving what God freely gives His sons. In the Kingdom, there are no ceilings, no limits to who we can become, how much we can heal, or how deeply we can know the Father. But those old ceilings don't fall without a fight. In the world, we're taught there's a cap on success, healing and restoration. Culture says, "This is just who you are. Be grateful you made it this far." But in the Kingdom, we don't settle. We press forward because there's always more in God.

"I press toward the mark for the prize of the high calling of God in Christ Jesus."- Philippians 3:14

That "high calling" doesn't end with a paycheck, platform, or a good relationship with your kids. It's a continual transformation into who God created you to be. One of the biggest ceilings I had to tear down was the lie that manhood means isolation. I lived like I was on my own. That mindset made me capable but shut off. I couldn't need anybody. I couldn't cry. I couldn't trust. But sons don't live that way. John 15:5 says, *"I am the vine, ye are the branches… for without me ye can do nothing."* Jesus wasn't rebuking us He was reminding us: you were never created to carry it all alone. Independence sounds

> INDEPENDENCE SOUNDS STRONG, BUT IN THE KINGDOM, "DEPENDENCE IS STRENGTH"

strong, but in the Kingdom, "dependence is strength". In my old life, weakness was something to avoid. Now I know that God meets me in it. I don't have to perform for Him; I just have to be present with Him. There's no ceiling when you're living from a place of surrender. 2 Corinthians 12:9 says, *"My grace is sufficient for thee: for my strength is made perfect in weakness."* When I bring Him my brokenness, He brings me His strength. That's Kingdom exchange and it's how healing continues. God didn't just stop at saving me. He's still growing me, shaping me, and calling me higher. What I thought was the "top", peace with my dad, reconnection with my son was just the starting point of deeper healing. The Kingdom life doesn't peak. It progresses. From glory to glory. From one healed place to another. No ceilings, just deeper sonship. As I rebuild, I have to be intentional. Those old thoughts still knock telling me to toughen up, stay guarded, keep proving myself. But I've learned that those old blueprints can't be

> THE KINGDOM DOESN'T RECYCLE TRAUMA, IT REDEEMS IT

used in a Kingdom house. God is doing something new, and I must choose to build with Him. To truly build something lasting, I can't bring the old ceilings into the new house. Not for me. Not for my sons. The Kingdom doesn't recycle trauma, it redeems it.

What No Ceilings Look Like

- You pursue healing even when you're the only one who sees the wounds.

43

- You model love even when you didn't receive it the way you needed.

- You keep growing because you're no longer afraid to be led.

In the Kingdom, ceilings are only imaginary. The only limits are the ones we keep trying to rebuild. But if we let Him, God will tear them all down and show us how to live like sons with no ceilings, only grace.

CHAPTER 7

THE STRENGTH OF BEING SEEN

How Vulnerability Transforms Fatherhood and Marriage

Rebuilding is messy work. No one tells you that healing comes with grief. That every step forward in wholeness reveals another layer of brokenness still hiding beneath. It wasn't until I started building my life on God's truth, a foundation of grace, His presence, and my identity in Him, that I realized I was still emotionally unstable in some areas. It started with small things like a TV commercial; a father hugging his son after a game. It was a movie scene where the dad shows up when it matters most. I'd be in tears. And not just tears, wounded, hurtful, soul-deep cries I didn't know I still had in me. I'm a grown man, a father, a provider, a protector. I know the truth. I had forgiven my father. I had reconciled with him. I understand that God is Father above all. And yet... my heart still longed for what my natural father couldn't give me. That longing didn't go away with age or knowledge. It just sat quietly, waiting for the right moment to surface. The deeper I leaned into the reality of being a son of God, the more I recognized what I had missed out on as a child. And those unmet needs began to leak into my own parenting. I began to project my emotional wounds onto my son.

He didn't call enough. He didn't show enough gratitude. He didn't run toward our relationship with the urgency I thought it deserved. I wanted him to do everything I thought I would have done if my father had been present. If I had the chance he had. But the truth is, I don't know what I would have done. I only know what I feel I would have done and I was using those feelings to define what my son should be doing. Unintentionally, I was placing an emotional burden on him that didn't belong to him. I was trying to relive my story through him, not realizing that this, too, was a ceiling. A ceiling built on emotional expectation instead of kingdom truth.

> I HAD TO BE EMOTIONALLY HONEST AND SPIRITUALLY SURRENDERED

I was also seeing it in how I handled his younger siblings. I was more present and more engaged. But I was impatient. The emotional frustration I had with my oldest son, whom I wanted to "get it" was showing in how I dealt with my younger sons and daughter. I was unintentionally creating a comparison. Not a visible one. But one that subtly showed up in my tone, in my disappointment, in my quick corrections. I had to stop. I had to remember what God reminded me of in this process:

"Casting all your care upon him; for he careth for you."
—*1 Peter 5:7 (KJV)*

God wasn't asking me to suppress my emotions. He was asking me to submit them. Not to stuff them down, but to give them over. I couldn't let my wounds drive my parenting. I had to be emotionally honest and spiritually surrendered. My emotions weren't wrong, they just weren't Lord. In this part of the rebuild, God showed me that even though the foundation is new, my heart needs constant guarding. The ceilings I once broke through don't rebuild themselves, but the old materials are always nearby. Emotional instability was one of those materials. And if I'm not careful, I'll use them without realizing it. I don't want my children...any of them to feel like they have to become who I never got to be. That's not their burden. That's not their call. And it's not their job to heal what I still mourn. Only God can do that. This part of the rebuild reminds me that being a healthy father isn't just about showing up. It's about being whole while I do. And when I'm not, I need to be honest about it. I'm still healing. Still growing. Still learning how to cry without shame and love without strings. And that, too, is part of the kingdom floor: no ceilings on healing. No limits on how deeply God can father me.

When Strength Looks Like Weakness

The deeper I went into this rebuild, the more I began to realize I wasn't just renovating how I fathered, I was being called to renovate how I loved. Especially how I loved my wife. I used to think vulnerability was for prayer time. That God was the only one I was supposed to pour my heart out to. And in a way, that made sense. In prayer, I found safety. In worship, I found expression. In Scripture, I found identity. But when it came time to sit across from my wife and express the same emotions I gave to God, I struggled. I didn't realize how emotionally unstable I had become, not just as a father, but as a husband. The new layers of brokenness that were being uncovered as I stepped into true sonship had ripple effects and those ripples were crashing into my marriage. I would come home and feel something stirring inside, sadness, disappointment and fear, but when she asked, "What's wrong?" I gave the usual answers: "I'm good." "Nah, nothing." "I'm just tired." Passive responses that turned the conversation away. I told myself I was protecting her. That it was my job to carry the weight, not to burden her with it. But deep down, I was protecting myself from being seen, from being questioned and from being misunderstood. I've always been the funny one. The encourager. The guy who lightens the room with a joke or a smile. But God showed me something heavy: those laughs, those smiles, they were a shield. A deflection. A way of staying surface-level even while claiming to be "present."

"Two are better than one... For if they fall, the one will lift up his fellow: but woe to him that is alone when he falleth." —Ecclesiastes 4:9-10 (KJV)

I didn't realize how alone I was emotionally, not because my wife wasn't there, but because I wasn't letting her in. I had spent so much time trying to be a rock that I didn't notice I was becoming emotionally distant. And ironically, the very vulnerability God had been teaching me to embrace as His son was the same vulnerability I was withholding from my wife. What I thought was protection was actually isolation. This wasn't about her not being trustworthy. This was about me learning to be fully known without shame. Because the truth is, vulnerability with God is safe because He already knows everything. But vulnerability with a spouse? That requires courage. It requires honesty. It requires trust. And not just trust in her, but trust in who God says I am. That I'm still loved when I'm not strong. I am still respected when I'm broken. I am still covered when I'm naked. Genesis 2:25 says, "And they were both naked, the man and his wife, and were not ashamed." That's what vulnerability in marriage should look like. A restored perspective of Eden, where naked doesn't mean weak. It means safe. I wasn't modeling that well. I wanted to be affectionate, loving, and attentive without appearing weak.

I thought showing weakness would invite concern or cause worry. But I'm learning that the lack of vulnerability promotes distance. It builds walls. It says, "I'm fine without you," even when I'm not. And those unspoken walls don't just affect my marriage. They spill over into how I handle my children. My emotions toward my oldest son, those moments of sadness that turn into impatience, and the desires I tried to push onto him, those were a direct reflection of emotions I hadn't shared or processed with the one person God gave me to walk this road with. I learned vulnerability is strength when it's done in love. God didn't just ask me to weep in the prayer closet. He asked me to be seen…fully seen ….by the one I've covenanted to walk with. To open the door to my emotions, not so she can fix me, but so we can walk together. That's what covering looks like. Not hiding. But being open under grace. Healing happens in connection. Growth happens in honesty.

> THE LACK OF VULNERABILITY PROMOTES DISTANCE. IT BUILDS WALLS. IT SAYS, "I'M FINE WITHOUT YOU," EVEN WHEN I'M NOT

And the man I'm becoming isn't one who just leads in strength but, one who leads in transparency. So now, when the tears come, I don't hide them. When the hurt hits, I talk about it. When the weight gets heavy, I let her help me lift it. That's not weakness…it's kingdom partnership. And in this rebuild, I'm realizing: the same way I've been learning how to be a son to God, I'm also learning how to be a husband to my wife. One who isn't afraid to be seen, even in the cracks.

THIS ISN'T ABOUT DENYING THAT I FEEL. IT'S ABOUT REFUSING TO LET FEELINGS DEFINE MY IDENTITY OR DIRECT MY DECISIONS

I'm learning now more than ever, that while I must be honest about my emotions, I can't be led by them. For most of my life, emotions were either suppressed or explosive. Either I buried them deep, thinking that was strength, or I let them guide me, especially the anger and hurt I carried from my father's absence. Neither of those paths were healthy, and neither of them reflected who I truly am in Christ. But now, through sonship, I'm discovering a third way: acknowledging my emotions, while being led by truth.

"He that is slow to anger is better than the mighty; and he that ruleth his spirit than he that taketh a city." —Proverbs 16:32 (KJV)

This isn't about denying that I feel. It's about refusing to let feelings define my identity or direct my decisions. My wife and children don't need a perfect man. They need a present one. One who can admit, "I'm hurt," or "I'm confused," or even "I am wrong," but who also says, "Let's pray," or "Let me think on this," instead of lashing out or shutting down. I used to think being a strong man meant being unshakable. Now I realize being a God-led man means being moldable. I've had moments, many in fact, where emotions tried to take the lead. When my oldest son didn't respond the way I hoped, I felt overlooked. When my younger children needed correction, I felt triggered. When my wife wanted to talk deeper, I felt cornered. And my reflex, at times, was to go quiet, go cold, or go into "fix-it" mode instead of leaning into God's presence for wisdom. Again, Romans 8:4 says, "For as many as are led by the Spirit of God, they are the sons of God." This verse doesn't say as many as are led by their emotions. It says sons of God are led by His Spirit. That's a truth I have to remind myself of daily. I can be real about how I feel but I must be rooted in who I am. That's the difference. God didn't just call me to be a son in private. He called me to be a son in front of my family. That means my household gets to see what grace under pressure looks like. They see when I lose my temper and when I repent. They see when I wrestle emotionally and when I return to God's Word. They don't just see their father, they see a man being fathered.

"And have put on the new man, which is renewed in knowledge after the image of him that created him." —Colossians 3:10 (KJV)

That's the man I'm becoming! One who doesn't live in emotional extremes. One who doesn't let old pain drive new decisions. One who remembers that just because emotions are present doesn't mean they're *in charge.* This process has revealed that the real strength of a man is not how much emotion he hides but how well he surrenders that emotion to God. Because my kids don't just need to see a strong dad. They need to see a surrendered one. And my wife? She doesn't just need security, she needs connection. Not a fortress to live with, but a partner to walk beside. This is how the rebuild deepens: not just tearing down the old walls of "You're on your own," but refusing to let emotions build new ones. In this house, I'm not just a leader. I'm a living example of what it looks like to follow. I follow Jesus. I follow truth. I follow love, even when it hurts. And when I do mess up...and I will...it's not the end. It's another invitation to bring my emotions back to the feet of my Father. Not to be shamed, but to be shaped. Because I am a son...not just when I'm strong, but especially when I'm still learning.

> MY KIDS DON'T JUST NEED TO SEE A STRONG DAD. THEY NEED TO SEE A SURRENDERED ONE

CHAPTER 8

REBUILDING FROM THE RUBBLE

Learning to Build Forward Without Reversing Time

B efore you can build forward, you have to stop trying to reverse time. That's one of the hardest lessons I've had to learn. When you're in the rubble of what you've torn down, it's tempting to try and reconstruct the past, piece by painful piece. But the truth is: God didn't call me to patch up my past. He called me to walk in the new. Still, I'd be lying if I said that was easy. As I began to rebuild my life as a father, a husband, and a son, I kept bumping into this heavy pressure to make up for lost time. I have been tempted to make up every missed moment with my children, every emotional wall with my wife, every reaction, every silence, every selfish choice. I wore my past like a weight. Not because someone else put it on me. But because I did. I know what I did. I know how distant I was. I know how many heart-to-hearts, and "I'm proud of you's" I left unsaid. And when you know the depth of your own mess, self-forgiveness can feel almost impossible. But it's not.

"There is therefore now no condemnation to them which are in Christ Jesus, who walk not after the flesh, but after the Spirit." — *Romans 8:1 (KJV)*

Condemnation is not God's voice. It sounds like mine. But it's actually the voice of the accuser replaying past failures in surround sound. And that voice doesn't lead to healing. It leads to hiding. It leads to performing. It leads to people-pleasing, which might look like love but, it's still a mask. Some days, I catch myself trying to "prove" that I've changed; trying to earn my eldest son's trust; trying to be that playful dad to win over

> THE GRIEF OF WHO I WAS WILL ALWAYS TRY TO COMPETE WITH THE GRACE OF WHO I'M BECOMING

the younger ones; trying to win my wife's affection; trying to be perfect, just to prove I'm no longer broken. But that's not what God asked of me. He never said, "Fix it all." He said, "Follow Me." This is a process. And if I don't give myself permission to walk it out, I'll abandon it out of guilt. The grief of who I was will always try to compete with the grace of who I'm becoming. I have to choose grace. Not to excuse the past but to stop living in it. I've also learned that while God's changing me, others are still adjusting to me. And that can be frustrating. Just because I've shifted doesn't mean people automatically know how to receive the new version of me. Some are still waiting for the old me to show up. Some might even prefer the old me because he was predictable, even if he was unhealthy. That kind of pressure can become an invitation to relapse; to be who people recognize instead of who

God's calling me to be. But I can't build forward while looking over my shoulder.

What I'm doing now is no longer for approval. It's out of obedience and sonship. And being a son means trusting that my Father God sees every step, even the ones no one else claps for. He sees the quiet apologies, the private prayers, and the small internal wins that no one notices but heaven. I also realize now that my desire for approval from others was in a way me wanting approval from my

> BUT NO ONE CAN FILL A FATHER-SIZED VOID BUT THE FATHER

father. I didn't get it then, so I looked for it in my wife, in my kids, in my ministry, in those who I grew close to. But no one can fill a father-sized void but the Father. I'm learning to lay down pity. To stop rehearsing how much I missed. I can mourn without being manipulated by memory. And I can accept that I may never be fully understood or accepted in this new chapter. That's okay. Because I'm not living for acceptance anymore…I'm living from it. God accepted me before I got it right. My identity as a son doesn't begin after I'm perfect. It began when I said yes. 1 John 3:2 says, *"Beloved, now are we the sons of God, and it doth not yet appear what we shall be…"* That's where I'm living now in the "not yet." I'm not where I was. I'm not yet who I'm becoming. But I'm right where God has me. And I'm learning to love this part of the process. No more self-pity. No more pressure to reverse time. Just steps. One after another.

One of the hardest things to do is slow down. It's not just that I want to make progress, it's that I want to fix everything now. I see the cracks in my foundation. I recognize the moments I missed with my children, the emotional withdrawal with my wife, and the silence I once carried in relationships that deserved more from me. And something in me screams: "Make it right before it's too late!" But I'm learning that urgency isn't always holy. Sometimes it's panic disguised as purpose.

> BUT I'M LEARNING THAT URGENCY ISN'T ALWAYS HOLY. SOMETIMES IT'S PANIC DISGUISED AS PURPOSE

The truth is, my rush to restore isn't just about today. It's rooted in yesterday. I didn't get my father when I wanted him. I didn't get the covering, the protection, or the pursuit I needed in the moments I needed it most. So now that I have the chance to give what I never received, there's a pressure to do it all perfectly and quickly as if somehow that could heal the boy in me who waited too long. But just because I want fruit now doesn't mean the seed hasn't already been planted. It takes patience to see growth. And not just patience with others, patience with myself, and with God.

"But let patience have her perfect work, that ye may be perfect and entire, wanting nothing."—James 1:4 (KJV)

Patience is doing its work in me. And it's not passive, it's powerful. Patience isn't waiting around doing nothing. It's choosing to trust that God is doing something, even when I can't see it yet. It's trusting that the process He has me in is producing more than I realize. There's compatibility between patience with God and patience with myself. They work hand in hand. I can't claim to trust God's timing if I won't give myself room to grow. And I can't truly walk in grace toward others if I haven't allowed that grace to reach the unfinished places in me. I have to remind myself: just because I

> I CAN'T CLAIM TO TRUST GOD'S TIMING IF I WON'T GIVE MYSELF ROOM TO GROW

don't see the results yet doesn't mean the root isn't growing. Healing takes time. Growth takes consistency. Restoration takes the Spirit, not just speed. Galatians 6:9 says, *"And let us not be weary in well doing: for in due season we shall reap, if we faint not."* I don't want to faint. But I also don't want to forfeit this journey by rushing it. That's what self-pity tried to do, convince me that I had to fix everything or I'd never be free from my past. But freedom isn't earned through urgency. It's received through surrender.

Even in my relationships, I see how this pressure has leaked out. I've tried to expedite healing with my oldest son because I know the pain that distance causes. I didn't want him to experience what I did so I pressured him to respond to me in the way I would have responded to my father, if he had been present. But my son isn't me. He doesn't carry my wounds. And I can't force my healing onto his journey. Even with my younger children, I've felt impatient. I want to ensure they get the best version of me and wanting every moment to be a redeeming one. But if I'm not careful, I'll create new ceilings of performance, measuring their acceptance of me based on how quickly I become who I think I should be. And with my wife, I've seen how my silence or passivity was just another version of fear. I called it "being strong." I thought I was protecting her from my mess, when really I was protecting myself from the discomfort of being seen.

> FAITH DOESN'T RUSH. IT TRUSTS. IT PLANTS. IT WATERS. IT WAITS

Vulnerability with God took faith and humility, in a sense the same was required with her. It required honesty. And it required me to slow down, open up, and stay present. Faith doesn't rush. It trusts. It plants. It waters. It waits. And I'm learning through this that this walk from broken man to beloved son isn't about speed. It's about surrender.

God's not asking me to rewind time. He's asking me to walk with Him now. The places where I feel furthest behind are invitations to be led, not to overcompensate. The gaps I feel in relationships and in memory are not assignments to fix. They're altars. Places where I lay down my guilt and let God bring life again. So today, I breathe deeper. I rest more. I'm learning to trust God's pace. To give myself permission to be a work in progress. To relieve myself of the pressure to fix it all overnight. And to believe that the same God who was with me in my brokenness is with me in my building.

"Being rooted and built up in him, and established in the faith, as ye have been taught…"—Colossians 2:7 (KJV)

I'm rooted. I'm being built. And I'm not in a hurry. Because this time, I'm building to last.

CHAPTER 9

BUILDING BEYOND THE CEILINGS

When God Turns Our Limits Into Launchpads

If you've ever lived in a space with low ceilings, you know what it feels like. You duck your head. You move with caution. You avoid jumping too high. Eventually, you learn to live with the limit. That's what ceilings do, they restrict upward movement. Spiritually and emotionally, ceilings are just the same. I didn't realize how many ceilings I had built in my life until God started tearing them down.

- Ceilings of emotional restraint—"Men don't cry."

- Ceilings of independence—"You're on your own, so figure it out."

- Ceilings of comparison—"You'll never be better than your father was."

- Ceilings of performance—"If you don't do it right, you're not worthy of love."

Each of these was built brick by brick, often through pain, disappointment, and silence. They were my way of protecting myself. But over time, what I thought was protecting me was

59

actually containing me. I wasn't growing. I was surviving. I wasn't living as a son; I was living like a servant with something to prove. God didn't just point out these ceilings, He walked me through their demolition. And He did it with patience, tenderness and truth. He showed me the emotional ceiling, the times I cried over a father-son scene on TV, overwhelmed by the grief of not having that closeness myself. That wasn't weakness, it was the Holy Spirit bringing up what I buried so He could heal it. He revealed the relational ceiling in my marriage when I realized I was withholding vulnerability, thinking strength meant silence. But in God's Kingdom, strength looks like surrender. He called me to show my wife not just my strength but my struggle. He shattered the fatherhood ceiling when I tried to force healing with my son based on my own pain, not his process. I wanted him to do what I wished I had done with my dad, call more, hug longer, stay closer. But that's when God reminded me: "Let Me be his Father too. You're not rebuilding alone." One by one, the ceilings cracked. And beneath the debris, I discovered something holy: foundation. A place to build again but this time, without the limits of my past.

All of it started with a submitted yes. Not just a yes to change, but a yes to the leadership of Jesus. Without Him, none of this would be possible. He's the one who never left. The one who saw the broken places and stayed anyway. He didn't just give me a new language; He gave me a new life. Through His sovereignty and mercy, I've been invited into a new way of being a son first, before a father. That has changed everything. It redefined manhood, not by strength alone, but by surrender. I've learned that healing doesn't happen in a rush, and growth isn't always loud. Sometimes, it's slow. Sometimes, it hurts. But it's always worth it. There were times when I wanted to go back to what was familiar, to what others expected, to what was easier. But I can't unsee what God has shown me: His way is better, and my story surrendered to Him can be used to build something eternal.

> I'VE LEARNED THAT HEALING DOESN'T HAPPEN IN A RUSH, AND GROWTH ISN'T ALWAYS LOUD. SOMETIMES, IT'S SLOW. SOMETIMES, IT HURTS. BUT IT'S ALWAYS WORTH IT

Now I understand: **When ceilings become floors**, it's not just about me getting free. It's about laying down something others can rise from. My sons, my daughter, my marriage, and even the men reading this…this floor is for us all.

I used to think growth meant pushing through pain and proving myself worthy. But now I see growth in the Kingdom begins with surrender. Ceilings fall when I say yes, not to my own strength, but to the strength of Jesus. The rebuilding hasn't been instant. It's been slow, intentional, and sacred. But with each "yes" I've given Him…

- The yes to forgive what felt unforgivable.

- The yes to pursue my son without forcing outcomes.

- The yes to change how I relate to my younger children.

- The yes to be vulnerable with my wife.

- The yes to be led by God, not my emotions.

- The yes to stay when self-pity said go.

- The yes to patience, even when I wanted quick results.

…God has been crafting a new floor beneath my feet.

This floor wasn't built in a day and definitely not in a classroom. It was built in the middle of my mess. In the breakdowns. In the quiet "God, am I even getting this right?" moments. It's a floor of wisdom I didn't start with because some things, you only learn by living through them. I learned by failing and by getting back up. This isn't the kind of wisdom that needs to be loud. It listens. It surrenders. It knows when to stop talking and just trust God. It's a floor of empathy that only pain could teach me. I didn't really understand what it meant to show up until I knew what it felt like to be left out. I didn't understand compassion until I realized how often I judged people without knowing their story. It's a floor of truth built on tears. Because pretending got exhausting. I had to stop acting like the little boy inside me wasn't still hurting. Still asking, "Why don't he want me?" The tears weren't a breakdown; they were a breakthrough. God used them to show me not just who my father was, but who I am and how much I still need His voice over mine. And it's a floor of grace, not because I crushed it, but because God covered it.

> THE TEARS WEREN'T A BREAKDOWN; THEY WERE A BREAKTHROUGH

Every time I lost my cool. Every time I slipped back into old habits. Every time I tried to build something on my own strength and failed, He laid down more grace. He covered the cracks. Made beauty out of what I wanted to hide. Now I get it: This is legacy. Not a perfect past. Not pretending to have it all together. But saying "yes" when everything in me wanted to stay stuck. Saying "yes" to growth, to healing and to showing up even when it's uncomfortable.

So no…these aren't ceilings anymore. They are not ceilings of silence, shame or survival mode. They're floors of truth, healing, and hope. Floors my kids can stand on, not walls they have to break through. These are floors made of presence, not performance offering a freedom to be human, to feel, to fail, and still be fully loved. That's what it means when we say: **"Fatherhood: When Ceilings Become Floors."**

….So, to every man out there who feels like it's too late, too broken, or too far gone, hear me: IT'S NOT. Start with a yes. One honest, surrendered yes to Jesus. Let Him do the building. He knows how to turn rubble into something holy.

ENDING PRAYER- A YES TO THE REBUILD

Father,

Thank You for being patient with me through the years I didn't see You, through the seasons I tried to build on brokenness, and even in the moments I thought I had to do it all alone. Today, I surrender. I give You my yes. Not just to be changed but to be rebuilt. To be made whole.

Lord, reveal every ceiling I've built, those formed in pain, in pride, in fear, and in survival. Show me the limits I've accepted as normal. Expose the lies I've believed about what it means to be a man, a father, and even a son. And when You show me those ceilings, give me the courage to let them fall.

Tear down what needs to be torn down. I don't want to carry what You never called me to carry. I don't want to build what You never asked me to build. Help me to trust You with the rubble. Help me to trust You with the slow, sacred process of healing. Give me the strength to show up, soft, surrendered, and available. Let my story become a floor someone else can stand on.

Thank You for being a Father who never left. Thank You for seeing me, claiming me, and calling me to more. I believe You can restore everything I lost. I believe You can father me while You teach me how to father others. I give You my heart. I give You my story. I give You my yes.

In Jesus' name,

Amen.

WAYS TO IDENTIFY HIDDEN CEILINGS IN YOUR LIFE

1. Your Definition of Success Is Rooted in Proving Someone Wrong- *If your drive comes from trying to outdo your father's failures or prove your worth, it's likely a ceiling built from pain or rejection.*

2. You Struggle to Receive Love Without Earning It- *If compliments, rest, or kindness make you uncomfortable unless you've "performed well," you may have built a ceiling of performance-based identity.*

3. You Avoid Vulnerability, Even with Those Closest to You- *When opening up emotionally feels like weakness or danger, it's often a sign of a ceiling formed by past hurt or neglect.*

4. You Parent From Pain Instead of Wholeness- *If you're overly strict, over-giving, or emotionally distant with your kids to "fix" what you lacked, you may be unknowingly building from brokenness.*

5. You Struggle to See God as a Loving Father- *If your prayers are transactional or filled with guilt, not connection, you might still be viewing God through the ceiling of your earthly father's behavior.*

6. You're Afraid to Ask for Help or Show Weakness- *A strong show of independence is often a ceiling labeled as strength but rooted in fear of disappointment or rejection.*

7. You Celebrate Doing "Better Than Your Dad" but Still Feel Empty- *Beating the past doesn't equal healing. If you've made progress but still feel a void, it could be because the ceiling wasn't just an achievement…it was internal.*

8. You Often Say Things Like:

   o *"I'll never be like him…"*

   o *"I just have to figure it out myself…"*

   o *"I'm not really the emotional type…"*